Like
Ripples
In A Pond

*Chronicles of the Family
of Hulda and Louis Stum*

P. K. ARBEGAST

Like Ripples in a Pond
Trilogy Christian Publishers A Wholly Owned Subsidiary of Trinity Broadcasting Network
2442 Michelle Drive Tustin, CA 92780

Cover design by: __

For information about special discounts for bulk purchases, please contact Trilogy Christian Publishing.

Manufactured in the United States of America
10 9 8 7 6 5 4 3 2 1
Library of Congress Cataloging-in-Publication Data is available.
ISBN: 978-1-68556-074-4
E-ISBN: 978-1-68556-075-1Dedication

This book would not be complete without the help of each family member and the delicious family recipes we all have shared over the years. Many recipes were handed down from Grandmother Johnson, who passed away before she was fifty, leaving ten children. Boots and Duane were the only two grandchildren born at the time of her death. Boots has fond memories of Grandmother Johnson. Our mother was the oldest child and had two children of her own but managed to take food to her siblings and nurture them with her love. Many of her brothers and sisters have gone on before her, but the remaining two sisters and two brothers are precious to us, and we pray for God's blessings upon them.

Our family is one of a kind, and I believe we have each been given a great gift of love and caring for each other as well as those who cross our paths along the way. As family members, share the love you have been given and find peace from within, as God has granted each of us.

I feel like Mother left each of us with a part of her that will never pass away.

With awesome love for all,

—Pat (Patty) Patricia Arbegast

3

Table of Contents

Introduction

Like ripples in a pond, our large family grew in many directions over the years, but we always will remember our roots of love and compassion, nurtured by our mother and sought after from our father.

Chapter 1

We had just been moved into the small farmhouse in Walnut Bottom, a very dark and dreary house with yellowing water-stained wallpaper in every room. The unmistakable odor of dust and mold permeated our nostrils as we walked through the front door clinging to Mom's skirt. There was no electricity or plumbing, but it was what Grandfather Stum had purchased for my mother and her five children, ages one to thirteen. Grandpa was concerned that we lived so far away from him and Grandma, and this house was available and affordable, as well as convenient for them to lend Mother a hand with the children.

Our grandparents stayed silent about our plight of moving from one house to another until we landed in the small cottages near New Kingstown. These tiny one- or two-roomed cabins were meant to be for vacationers, but we were able to secure temporary shelter through the cabin owner and found that, at least, we were all together in one place. The boys slept on the floor, while Boots had a cot, and Lonnie and I slept in dresser drawers! Lonnie was a tiny baby, so it was not a problem for him to snuggle up with the blankets and go to sleep. I was a frail two-year-old, so I could climb into the bottom drawer, lined with a blanket, and pray that nobody would close the drawer while I slept. (Please, do not try this method of sleep or play for your child. It is unsafe to do so and may cause injury to a child.) It was home, and Mom cooked what she could on a one-burner hot plate, a disaster waiting to happen, but, again, God was with us.

However, when World War II began to require all eligible men to be drafted, our father went willingly, leaving behind a devoted wife and five children. Our mother did not drive at the time, but we did have a car, which our grandfather brought to the farmhouse to be parked.

Dad (Louis) had been drafted into the Navy and sent for basic training in the Great Lakes of New York. We moved from our home in Bumble Bee Hollow, and before that, from a house sitting on the banks of the Susquehanna River in Enola. From Enola, we could hear the wail of the sirens in Harrisburg, across the Susquehanna River, and watch the city go dark in anticipation of an air raid from the German or Japanese aircraft; after all, it was wartime. My memories are vivid about this traumatic drama where we all had to hide under the table, eyes shut tight, hug our brother or sister, and await the sirens to sound the all-clear.

Our parents struggled to put food on the table, so the rent sometimes went unpaid, and we could not afford to own a house. Dad was a painter and decorator before the war, and he had to travel to where the job site needed to be done. Dad worked for Uncle Bob Jones, who was so good to us, but the painters all worked very hard, painting inside and outside, during the scorching hot summers and sometimes in very cold and cramped conditions in the winter. Dad had an artist's flair for his work and would balance two brushes of differing sizes in his left hand, between two fingers, while he mathematically scaled the scaffold and bathed the walls in refreshing new paint with a four-inch brush, using his right hand. His farmer's skin was tanned leather brown after an outdoor summer's work, and there was never a burn even without such a thing as sunblock.

Chapter 2

After Boots was born, Mom and Dad moved quite often, so Boots had to help with the chores as soon as she became old enough to assist. Her fond memories of going to Caledonia to visit one of Mom's Perry aunts remained etched in her mind. (Hulda's mother's maiden name was Perry.) This aunt and uncle were instrumental in nurturing Boots and comforting Mom in her early days of parenthood. These relatives lived in a magnificent, large Victorian house with a lush green manicured lawn. Boots loved playing on the soft grass with other cousins and relatives who were also visiting, and our family always enjoyed going to Caledonia Park for picnics in later years. As a child of about eight or nine years old, Boots cut asparagus for a neighbor lady where we lived at the time, and the lady was so gracious and thankful for this tiny girl's dedicated work ethic that one day she asked Boots which one of the cocker spaniel puppies, who were then about eight weeks old, would she like to have to take home. Their names were Peggy and Polly. Boots' choice was Polly, so off she went toward home, carrying her bundle of happiness. She was so excited to show Mom and Dad this darling little pitch-black, curly-haired puppy with the cutest little pink tongue and tiny paws. We all loved Polly, who was well mannered and disciplined. As we all grew up, Polly too became older and slower with age. Back in the day…dogs were not permitted in the house, so Polly stayed on the front porch all night, except when very cold weather struck and Mom would let her come inside and sleep by the stove for warmth. When Polly was about fourteen or fifteen years old, for some strange reason, she found comfort under Dad's car at night. One morning, Dad got into his car and began to back up to go to work when he realized he had run over our precious Polly. Dad was upset and sort of apologized to Polly by saying he did not know she was under the car. There was not a dry eye in the entire household for several days after Polly was gone. It still fills my heart with sadness when I remember the day we lost Polly; she was just so very special.

Duane was born after Mom and Dad moved to Hockersville, near Walnut Bottom. Duane was sick a lot and could not tolerate milk, so Grandpa Stum (Jim) came to visit and brought Horlick's Malted Milk, reminding Mother if she did not get some of this milk substitute into Duane, he was going to die. Mother followed Grandpa's instructions, and Duane soon became healthy and was thriving with energy to help with the family chores.

During this time, Dad would come home from painting all day and wash the paint off with gasoline. One night, Dad sat the kerosene lantern beside him in order to see where the paint had splashed on his arms and face, and the gas caught fire and severely burned his arms and hands. Dad recovered but, of course, was unable to work for quite a while, so, once again, we were forced to move.

Our next stop was in Boiling Springs, where Lou was born, and Grandma Johnson (our mother's mom) passed away at the farm where she lived with Grandfather and their nine children. The youngest child was four years old at the time. Our mother knew the night she lost her mother because a dog had howled all night near the house, and she received the message of her mother's death the following morning. Mom was very intuitive and followed the prodding of the Holy Spirit to grieve personally and quietly alone. Mom never really accepted the fact that she no longer had her mother to lean on for help in raising the children, so, once again, the Perry family came to the rescue; Aunt Florence, Aunt Edna, and Aunt Violet were a source of comfort and strength during these years.

Chapter 3

We then moved to Bumble Bee Hollow in Lower Allen, where I (Pat) and Lonnie were born. How did our poor mom and dad handle so many babies and children? It is miraculous that we all were nurtured and cared for by so many loving neighbors, friends, and, of course, relatives. Our survival was dependent on the loving prayers of our extended family members, who had many issues pertaining to the economically depressed situations of the day.

Apparently, Dad's artistic talent was passed onto some of his children and grandchildren—a magnificent legacy. One granddaughter is a world-renowned street chalk artist, along with her husband and sister. (You can visit their website at Tracy Lee Stum.com.)

Daddy's loyalty to the Painters and Decorators Union helped him to get meaningful employment, such as painting the tunnels for the Pennsylvania Turnpike, schools, and hospitals, but being in the Union came with a cost. Even when there were no jobs available during the winter months, Daddy was required to attend Union meetings and pay his dues. Mother made sure we were all ready to go along to the meetings when Dad arrived home. You see, Mother would sit in the car with at least four or five kids, scrapping and arguing, while Dad attended the meeting. Mother taught us to sing songs and motivated us to spell new words. The streets in the city (Harrisburg) were dark and unwelcoming, few people walked past, and alley cats came and left, looking for food. We stayed in the car, waiting and hoping we would at the very least get an ice cream cone on the way home. It rarely ever happened, but at least Mother made sure our dad got home safely.

After the war, when work was scarce, the blessed people of Walnut Bottom and Rehoboth Church contacted Dad to paint their homes and especially the Methodist Church. Although Dad never attended the church, he was always eager to paint and detail the sanctuary with great care and skill. When we went to services on Sunday morning, the church was sparkling with new paint and gleaming stained-glass windows. The aroma of paint lingered, but it always appeared the worshipers sang more clearly and prayed more loudly, with pride and thanksgiving. The money Dad received supplemented the Painters and Decorators Union pittance he received every other week, so the church pay was certainly a gift from God.

Grandma and Grandpa (Ella and Jim Stum) had lived

at the large farm that sat back a lovely, long dirt lane, lined with maple trees, clover, and honeysuckles blooming all summer. This farm was situated behind the small farm they later purchased and moved into since their children were married and gone from the home.

The sweet smell of new-mown hay permeated the nightly air as our cousins, Gladys Jones and Norma Heberlig, convinced their mothers to let them stay over for a few days with Aunt Ella and Uncle Jim "on the farm." Boots (my oldest sister) would also stay sometimes and loved the special attention from her grandma's German nurturing.

During winter nights when the girls would sleep over, Grandma heated irons, which were real flatirons (not electrified) on the woodstove, and wrapped them in towels to prevent burns, then neatly placed the wrapped irons at the foot of the bed to keep the girls warm since the farmhouse bedrooms were not heated. The little visitors, including Phyllis Wolfe (Givler), helped with the barnyard chores and were often chased back to the house by the overprotective goose at the chicken house every chance the goose saw to nip at the girls' ankles. Phyllis was also known for walking barefoot through the barnyard and giggling with laughter when the manure squished between her toes. I'm sure Aunt Ella and her own mother, Aunt Sarah, were not giggling when she arrived at the back door of the house, smelling and looking like she had been romping in the barnyard with the pigs and cows. Aunt Sarah, however, was always the jolly, lovely woman who was so deliriously happy to have a little girl like Phyllis that I don't remember ever hearing a sharp word from her regardless of the antics of Phyllis during these episodes.

Aunt Sarah lived in Carlisle and was very active in St. Paul's Lutheran Church as well as volunteering at the Carlisle Hospital. So, when the church had a rummage sale, Aunt Sarah always brought lovely dresses and shoes to Ella's house, where Boots and I would try things on. The dresses were magnificently stylish and so amazingly ornate that Boots and I felt as though we had been elevated to a luxurious mantle of precocious opulence. The soft pinks and blues of the flowing fabric in each article of clothing surrounded our bodies like a fluffy cloud of angel dust. Aunt Sarah was the most loving, affectionate, and caring lady I had ever met, and she will live on in my heart forever. Aunt Sarah passed away at the young age of fifty-six, and Phyllis has carried on her legacy of service through her registered nursing career as a nursing home administrator and serving South Middleton Township on the Planning Commission, as well as many commitments to her church. A lovely, dedicated professional in the true German stature of our ancestry.

Chapter 4

I don't know how we survived until our Stum Grandparents took over and brought us to the horrid farmhouse. Our grandparents were German immigrants and very strict in their housekeeping, farming duties, and discipline. In fact, the story remains that our great-great-grandfather Samuel Throne was born on a ship coming to America, and when he was grown became a Pvt. in Co E, 101 Reg. Pennsylvania Volunteer in the Civil War. A photo of this handsome man in full Union uniform has been given to me, which I will cherish. Duane, my oldest brother, bears a very strong resemblance to his great-great-grandfather. Apparently, this legacy of dedication through the military was handed down through the generations to Dad (Navy), his brother Kenneth (Army), Duane (Navy), Lonnie (Air Force), Richard Jones (Navy), Robert Jones (Navy), Leon Jones (Navy), Jennifer (Stum), Elliott (Army). Of course, there was also John Baum (Boots) (Air Force) and Larry Mathna (Vicki) (Navy) on the Stum side of the family, as well as Uncle Jack Johnson (Army), Uncle Norman Johnson (Army), Uncle Gene Heller (Erma) (Army), and Neil Stum (Betty) (Army), as far as I can recall. Apologies to anyone I missed, but we, of course, had many nieces and nephews who have served, and our pride is beyond words for all. Thank you for your service to this beautiful country—The United States of America. Brian McCurdy (Amy's ex-husband) proudly serves in the Air Force Band and is often a clarinet soloist for the Band's magnificent concerts. A must-see if you have the opportunity.

Folklore has it, and we have not been able to confirm, but it appears that Henry Stum (my great-great-grandfather) took up residence near New Germantown in Pennsylvania after arriving in America as a stowaway on a cargo ship from Germany and had a Native American lady as his wife.

The children in this family were: Edgar Henry Stum, John Stum, Cyrus Stum, Ann, Ell(en), Carry, James, and Elizabeth. Some stories surfaced naming Henry Old Indian Joe, and he apparently had some sort of general store. Again, I have not been able to verify Henry's wife's name. However, after some research of the northcentral area of Pennsylvania, I discovered the Susquehannock tribe as well as a small village where Iroquois Native Americans lived and nurtured the valleys of central Pennsylvania. Unfortunately, the natural woods and forests were decimated by the logging industry from the northern part of Pennsylvania. The land was cleared of forests and vegetation, which held the earthen soil together. Waterways and streams were rerouted and forced to pond north and west of the villages. After much rain and melting snow, the rivers became ravaging forces driving the water south and east, flooding the villages, which forced the inhabitants to move further north to New York State. A very disturbing story in the name of progress. The full account of this disturbing time in Pennsylvania can be found on the Pennsylvania Department of Conservation and Natural Resources website. The documentary is a very eye-opening drama demonstrating the resilience of native peoples in the region.

Chapter 5

Our grandparents' small farm across the creek from our home was always tidy and neat. The house perched on the hill was a small two-bedroom bungalow, painted snowy white, with a large front porch and handrails covered with roses and soft clusters of baby's breath, with trails of mock orange fluttering in the breeze.

The sweet aroma of rosewater drifted from the hand soap and washbasin sitting just inside the door. Grandma and Mother both made homemade soap, but a store-bought cake of soap always was used for bathing and female handwashing. Fragrance could be added to the homemade mixture of some very stringent ingredients for the soap but was rarely available for the ordinary farm women. What the homemade soap did to the skin was unmerciful and only used when absolutely necessary, but it sure did whiten the sheets and towels to a fanciful look of new.

The washstand just inside the door showcased a blue enamel basin and matching pitcher, and a chair sat next to it for Grandpa to remove his shoes after being outside most of the day. This area of the house was known as the wash house, and shoes were removed in this section before one could enter the main rooms. There were always fresh flowers blooming profusely from Grandma's spectacular gardens in the summer, creating a relaxing aroma from the honeysuckle and peonies growing close by. A huge oak tree sheltered the small white house through all kinds of weather, and the pines whistled in the night winds. The windows were opened during the summer to let the aromatic radiance of Grandma's flowers permeate the house. When it became unbearably hot, the house's windows were closed, blinds lowered, and curtains drawn to combat the stinging rays of the sun from early morning until dusk. It was calm and quiet inside while the inhabitants rested during the hot afternoon hours. (No air conditioners for the hot and weary farmers.)

Our grandparents had farm animals, of which there were three cows for milk and butter, as well as chickens for eggs. Ah yes, and then there were the aprons worn by all the ladies to cover their "day" clothes and make them last longer. After all, the ladies only had about two or three dresses to wear on a daily basis, as well as one lovely Sunday dress, which was neatly washed and painstakingly ironed, always delicate flowers printed on the cotton material and trimmed at the collar with lace or ribbon. The apron, which was hung around the neck and tied in a neat bow in the back, served many purposes, such as gathering the eggs, cradling a sickly chick for warmth, lifting a hot skillet from the stove, or wiping away little tears and runny noses. When company came, the aprons were an ideal hiding place for shy children, and when removed, displayed a fine cotton or muslin dress, clean and unmarked from the chores of the day. Kindling was brought into the house from outside to start the evening fire for dinner and was loosely wrapped in the apron for transport. Mom would start the fire in the cooking stove and begin preparing the evening supper after a long day at the factory, slipping off her shoes and giving orders to each child, like the tender, loving general of the staff. We all knew to get started on the task assigned before our daddy came home, or there would be, as Mom called it, "Marching Orders," or else. We didn't want to find out what "or else" entailed, so there was no backtalk or dispute.

Occasionally, a chicken was caught on Saturday, "euthanized," and roasted for Sunday dinners. This was a process I could not be a party to since the head of the chicken was cut off on a tree stump, and the animal fluttered around unmercifully until it died. The bird was then soaked in a large container of hot water, and the smelly thing then had its feathers plucked and singed over an open flame to remove the pin feathers. To this day, Boots does not eat chicken.

The animals were always tended at 6 a.m. and 6 p.m. and bedded for the night. Grandma gathered the eggs daily and occasionally would "set" a hen—let the hen keep her eggs and hatch chicks for the next brood. It was so exciting to watch the eggs carefully, although we were not permitted to disturb the hen, and then when the chicks would hatch, Grandma would always call us over to her farm to see the baby chicks. As always, though, the chicks had to be carefully tended and held within a fence to protect them from the fox that would prowl at night. As the chickens grew, their wings were clipped at the ends so they could not fly over the fences, and it worked. This, supposedly, did not harm the chicken.

Chapter 6

Grandpa Stum worked on the farm in the mornings, then went off to work with Huge McCullough stringing the Newville phone company, which they co-owned, throughout the day. Grandma was the only person in our community to have a phone. It was a wall-mounted crank to get an operator, speak into the little horn-shaped speaker, then listen through the earpiece model, which antique dealers would die for today. The operator at the phone company was alerted when the phone was cranked to ring a bell. She was pleasant and would plug in the proper wires on her end to connect the two parties. The phone was so lovely with the polished hardwood and brass accents, but then, everything in Grandma's house was perfect in my little eyes.

The gorgeous round mahogany claw foot dining table was always set for the next meal, including the butter dish, and of course, the homemade apple butter. Table service for two was set with a shiny black porcelain-handled knife, a fork, and a spoon, as well as a white ironstone coffee cup and saucer, in place for the next meal. Doilies were neatly starched and ironed for the middle of the table. Then, the table was neatly covered with a crisp, freshly ironed white linen cloth. Grandma even had running water from a tap in the kitchen, and Grandpa installed a very nice bathroom some years later. Such luxuries were not to be had in our house, however, for many years.

The bedrooms were magnificent in their placement of high carved headboards and little square side tables, of the darkest shiny hardwood, polished to perfection, covered with tiny lace doilies. The high beds were also covered in freshly washed (every Monday morning) and ironed linens, some with batik laced corners or decorated with fine needlepoint violets of varying shades of purple. A white linen starched and ironed bedspread was laid neatly on top of the bed with the lace top rolled down, permitting the crisp white bedsheets to peak through and puff up in anticipated pride for a long night's rest for the weary. It was an aura of elegance to take one's breath away when the unmistakable aroma of fresh air-dried linens with lavender clusters from the vase drifted by in the seductively tempting mirage of the ensuing twilight utopia.

We were only permitted to sneak a peek into these stately aromatic rooms of grand opulence and fine cut glass vases. When Grandma wasn't looking, I would garnish a glimpse. My eyes did not miss a thing, down to the two mahogany-framed, white-matted pictures of Momma and Poppa, as Grandma lovingly referred to her deceased parents, securely placed above the headboard of the statuesque bed in the guest room. Grandma always had a dish of Good & Plenty in her cupboard for the grandkids, but we were all shy and frightened to ask for some, so we always talked Lonnie into asking for the candy for all of us since Lonnie seemed to be Grandma's special grandchild…what a treasure.

I hope it is true that we can only remember the beautiful and loving things about our grandparents after they have departed this earth. Perhaps this, too, will be the legacy we all leave to our own grandchildren.

Our brothers, Duane and Louie, would work on the farm, particularly in the summer, to bale hay. Duane was always called to assist Grandma—she would call him from her huge white wrap-around front porch, and Duane would respond. Her usual "you-hoo" could be heard at our house, so we knew Grandma needed help in some way.

Sometimes the cows had escaped their fences, or Grandma needed someone to gather the eggs. Duane was the oldest son and would help to bring in the milk to the milk house for separation of the cream. Of course, the cream was a most valued commodity since it was the luscious, wonderfully creamy-white mixture Grandma would put into the wooden butter churn and turn the handle until it thickened and became the most marvelously delicious sweet butter, which was shared with our needy family. We only used enough butter on an ear of corn to give it a sweet, magnificent lather, of which the rich can only dream.

The Beidel's—now they were beloved neighbors—lived across the street from us, and Mr. Beidel was an engineer on the railroad. Mrs. Beidel, aka Beidel, worked in the Penn Pants Factory. They had two grown sons and two adult daughters, the youngest of which was finishing high school. One daughter worked in the factory, while the young one went into nursing. They were always there for us and shared homemade pot pie of the finest thin rolled dough and freshly baked walnut cake, topped with frosting dripping down the sides, as well as many other treats. Mrs. Beidel worked very hard in the sweaty, unbearably hot factory, so we all received new pajamas for Christmas. It was a very special gift since we usually received just a pair of mittens and some candy or another article of clothing, which was desperately needed. Mrs. Beidel was a committed Christian from deep in the south mountain, and when I was very sick with a case of impetigo, which had penetrated my bloodstream, Mother reluctantly spoke with Mrs. Beidel about needing help for me since the doctor's salve did not seem to diminish the pain. "Beidel" (Margaret) contemplated the request, then called me and Mother over to her front porch, where Mom and Beidel spoke softly and discussed the gift Mrs. Beidel had been blessed with for most of her life.

Beidel was able to eradicate the disease from my bloodstream by some form of speaking in tongues and placing her hands about an inch or two above my skin while I lay across her lap. She held a blue light over my decimated sick body and moved it as she spoke softly in this foreign tongue. I still marvel at her healing power over my ravaged body. We were told not to speak of this, which I have adhered to all these years. I think I was about four years old at the time, so perhaps that was my first realization of the power of our Creator. Beidel was the only person around the area that was able to render God's healing power in this manner, and she was completely exhausted by the time she was finished. I recovered rapidly and soon returned to singing and playing with my dolls. Healings of this nature were viewed with some skepticism and fear in that day since the mountain folk did not understand the power of God's healing. Today, I am humbled and in awe of the powerful gift given by our Heavenly Father to this tiny, round south mountain native woman manifested as our blessed neighbor. As I grew up, Mrs. Beidel would call me over to her house on Saturdays, and when she washed her hair, I would either pin up her hair with bobby pins or give her a perm, occasionally, so she could look her best for church services on Sunday. We all loved the Beidel family and their everlasting kindness to our family.

Chapter 7

Our Christmas tree was always cut the night before Christmas when Dad would go to the mountain and saw one down when he was not always in the best of moods. Regardless of how it looked, we decorated it with the large blue, green, red, and yellow string of lights and encircled the tree with paper garlands made in art projects at school by each of us. The magical scent of pine drifted through the house, and the excitement of Christmas was evident. Mother made delicate sugar cookies and her Norwegian/Finnish bread braid decorated with luscious creamy frosting drizzles and cherries on top. She hustled around the kitchen with her apron on and children eager to lick the bowls. Walnuts were cracked and picked from the shell for baking the magnificent walnut cakes. A turkey was prepared with all the trimmings of buttery mashed potatoes with gravy, corn fresh from the jar taken from the cellar, cranberry sauce with fresh apples and oranges, peas so green they appeared to be picked from the garden that very morning. There was always a banana salad (recipe follows) at each plate, and the table was so full of nuts and bread we had barely enough room to be seated, but oh, the aroma of the holiday dinner…the mincemeat pie, delicately filled with oranges, apples, lemon, beef and plenty of nutmeg and cinnamon contained just a splash of rum, which baked out anyway but left an intoxicating aroma when each slice of pie was cut. And then, the pumpkin pie with the flakiest pie crust was cut, and a large dollop of homemade whipped cream was centered on each piece. Hot coffee brewed in the percolator on the stove while everyone enjoyed the dinner and spoke of recent activities at school. Neighbors stopped by to chat and enjoy coffee and pie. What a wonderful memory, even though each child received only a pair of mittens or socks, an orange, and a little box of candies, usually from the church family.

Mother could pare the most incredible potatoes to be mashed. You see, she used a paring knife and peeled the skin from each potato. The peel or skin of the potato was as thin as tissue paper. The skin remained in one long spiral until she was finished with the entire potato. Mother prided herself on saving as much of the meat on the potato as possible, and try as I might, I am still unable to reach the level of perfection Mother achieved with just a knife. There were no instant potatoes on our table—never—and she would not have permitted them if they had even been invented.

Our doors were never locked, there was no need for a key, and neighbors and friends simply knocked and came on in to visit. Neighbors rarely ever went to visit anyone unless they also carried some homemade jam or jellies, a freshly baked pie, or perhaps a loaf of crispy, tan-crusted homemade bread. That's just how it was. Ah, such simpler times that I yearn for. We all knew everyone else in town, so there was no fear of robbery or vandalism; after all, we didn't have much to rob.

Chapter 8

With our father in the Navy and shipped to destinations such as Okinawa, we kept busy helping Mother. Dad wrote us letters as often as he could, telling us of crossing the Equator, being christened "A Neptune" (a naval ritual when crossing the Equator), and having to eat green spaghetti, as well as the unbearable heat on the deck of the ship, but his life was one of survival just as was ours back here in the States. When his ship was attacked and sunk, he and his fellow shipmates had to swim to the island where they were not greeted well by the natives. The natives were headhunters, and the mates had been warned of such ethnic celebrations. Dad and the other sailors learned new skills of survival by trying to communicate with the natives. In exchanging Navy rations and personal items for island-grown food and drink, the shipmates were taught how to make primitive jewelry and natural foods. Somehow, Dad survived and had many stories to tell when he was finally discharged in 1945.

During the war, our grandfather was busy at work, adding electricity to our farmhouse. Our mother solicited the help of the children who were old enough to tear off the dark, ugly wallpaper and add some paint to the walls. Mother directed, and Grandpa plowed the field to make a lovely garden of potatoes, corn, peas, beans, cabbage, and Duane even grew a crop of peanuts. Duane and Lou mowed the grass and tended our chickens.

Mother always cooked everything we were able to grow, and during summer vacation from school, Boots and I helped to "can" all the extra vegetables, stomp sauerkraut—which means you put the cabbage slaw in a crock, and, using a dowel, stomp the cabbage with added salt every so often until it begins to make juice and bubbles in the crock. This fermented in the cold cellar until winter when we would have pork, sauerkraut, and mashed potatoes. I'm sure Vicki and Becky had their turns helping in this procedure as they became old enough. Oh, how we hated being sent to that dark cellar to help with the canned goods! You know, giant spiders and creepy things!

The potatoes were picked from the field and stored in baskets in the cold cellar. Every Sunday, we had many family members visit for dinner, in which the stored vegetables and canned fruits were prepared and served with great pride. Of course, Saturdays were reserved for the girls to cook and bake delicious pies and cakes for such a large clan, and we loved it. The peach and apple pies were scrumptious, not to mention the Graham cracker pie made with custard filling, bananas on the bottom, and whipped cream neatly swirled on the top. The boys had a very difficult time staying away from the pies, and the lovely aroma of a freshly baked apple pie always commanded their attention. The creamed rice was always a family tradition and continues today, but the original rice was made with Grandma Stum's cream from her own cows. Who knew anything about pasteurization back then? Straight from the cow and into the "icebox" (another interesting concept).

The icebox was a small refrigerator in which the "iceman," who came to our house every Saturday, placed a huge cube of ice into the top portion of the refrigerator, which we know today as the freezer section. A pan was placed underneath the refrigerator, which caught the drips of water from the daily melting ice. This system kept the milk and meat cool, but who knows how many times the milk was on the verge of souring when we used it. Howbeit, with four growing boys, the milk never lasted much past breakfast cereal, and there was usually a "discussion" as to who used all the milk.

Grandpa and Grandma always provided us with fresh milk, usually every other day. The worst part of getting our milk from our grandparents was strawberry season when Mother made these delicious homemade shortcakes. We put them in a bowl, covered them with strawberries, and added the milk straight from the milk house. In the spring, Grandpa's cow grazed in the pasture during the day and ate an abundance of the fresh green, luxurious garlic, now growing rapidly in the fields. One bite of the strawberry shortcake with berries and a large splash of the "garlic" milk made me run from the table in distress. The garlic had penetrated the cow's milk and was just unfathomable to my taste buds, but then I was told I was just too picky... Yuk... My brothers laughed and ate my portion without a second thought.

The house was finally becoming livable, but since I was four years old, I was still so afraid of this dark, dreary house. It seemed unbearable to me, and my emotions were more than our poor mother could tolerate. Mom did not know how to deal with a child that cried all the time and did not realize that I was so very homesick for my Aunt Miriam and her family since they lived in Camp Hill in a beautiful home and had taken us into their home many times when my mother was overwhelmed with children and no income. Our aunts and uncles never hesitated to assist Mother by permitting one of us to visit their home for a week or two. However, we were expected to contribute to the family chores and did so without comment, even when Boots had to help clean the chicken houses with Aunt Fleta.

Mother continued to paint and repair the house on her own and made it as comfortable as possible. Grandma sewed the mattress ticking from material she purchased for pennies from the Newville Dress Factory into rectangular mattress covers. We, then, had to gather and sort hay from the field to stuff into the newly sewn cover, which would be placed on the beds as mattresses. It was interesting trying to get comfortable in a bed of straw, but it was quite warm in the winter when we awoke to snow on the inside of the window!

Winters were brutal, particularly when we were required to walk a half-mile each way to school, then home, and back at noon, after we ate our coffee soup for lunch. What a treat to have leftover cold morning coffee, lovingly poured over broken bread or crackers and topped with a spoonful of sugar and a smidgen of milk. It got us through the day at school. Oh, so nourishing too! Or perhaps the dish of the day was the leftover ham fat that had solidified and was now a lovely condiment for our sandwiches…no meat, just the fat and grease with what was known as ham jelly.

At dusk on Sunday night, Duane and Lou, who were now about nine and eleven years old, were required to take the large brown water boiler outside to the well and pump water until the boiler was three-quarters full. The boys would then have to carry the heavy boiler into the kitchen and place it on the coal stove to begin heating overnight for the Monday morning laundry.

Mother soaked the dirty clothes, sorted by color, in the washing machine tub, and hand-rubbed the socks and jeans on her scrubbing board, as it was called due to all the scrubbing. This was a ladder-shaped wood-framed piece about eighteen inches long, which was covered over and between the rungs with smooth metal, creating a groove between the rungs... You know, rub-a-dub-dub... I loved using that thing. There was no such thing as an electric washer and dryer, so the clothes were then rinsed in a clean tub of water and pushed through the two rubber spindles, which were cranked by hand, known as the ringer. This squeezed most of the water out of the clothes, and they were then ready to be hung on the many clotheslines assembled in the back yard, usually by 10 a.m. By evening, the clothes were usually dry, so Boots, Mom, and I removed the bright clean clothes and folded them neatly in the wash basket. The snowy white sheets were taken to the bedrooms to dress the beds in clean, fresh linens. Oh, how lovely the air-dried sheets smelled due to the hay and flowers growing nearby when we finally conceded to defeat from a long day, and we were soon fast asleep, stretched out on a fresh clean bed.

Mother talked Grandpa into teaching her how to drive and would use the car to take Grandma to church and for our weekly supply of what few food items we could afford, even getting a small sack of candy sometimes. Mother was finally getting a check from the Navy for our support, and she was a faithful and stringent money manager, paying the bills first, and if there was any money left, she would then buy one of us, perhaps, a pair of shoes from the five-and-ten-cent store.

What a treat to have a pair of new shoes, even if they made hideous blisters for the first several weeks, we tried not to complain. Most of the blisters were due to the socks that had been darned so many times to make them last longer... Mother would always treat our blisters and boo-boos before we went to bed with either whiskey and lily leaves or Pain King salve purchased from the Jewel Tea salesman who would stop by every home in the neighborhood, about once a month, to sell spices, teas, coffees, pain killers, pots and pans, silverware, candles, kerosene, and just about anything one needed. I loved to see all the items in the "tea man's" case and dreamed of having all those things someday. Then, we would have our nightly ritual of hearing the older children and Mom read the Bible to the younger children, prayers were said, asking our Heavenly Father to see us through and always to "bring Daddy home safely." Oh, the whiskey and lily leaves remedy was a tiny bit of whiskey in a bottle with petals from the daylilies added for soaking several months. This was strictly used for open wounds and cuts, and it sure did help the healing process...somehow! And we'd try not to get sick with bronchitis or a very bad cold because then we'd get a "plaster" (our own word), which consisted of a man's handkerchief or a large rag covered with Numotizine or Vicks Vapo Rub pasted to the neck and chest for comfort in breathing. Yuk, what a smell and how yukky it felt in the morning, but, again, it worked. Numotizine was a pink paste and became like plaster by morning, stuck to your chest, thus the analogy. Yowzer! Oh yeah, and we brushed our teeth with baking soda and went to an outhouse to use the "bathroom" although there was no taking of baths in this tiny house, which caused one to hurry back outside in order to breathe…heaven forbid when someone was sick…but it sure does make me appreciate my home with two bathrooms inside…

Daddy finally returned home from the war unharmed, and the family had a big celebration. He was so handsome in his Navy Blues, but I was so frightened of him since he had been gone so long. Boots was so happy to have him home and cherished the lovely ring he had made for her with a mother of pearl set. I, too, received a tiny ring, which I have kept with my most prized possessions all these years. Each child received a bracelet of finely carved metal with their name engraved into the top. Daddy had made these gifts for each of us while awaiting his rescue from the islands, along with the help of the native peoples. Priceless…

Mom and Dad struggled through the ensuing years to keep the family together, and we were all required to attend Sunday church services. Our grandmother became the youth group leader in the church—we never had a youth group until she and the minister established the most needed organization. Grandma was a wonderful teacher and Christian leader. Mother made sure we were always in attendance for all church activities, even when she now had three little children who tended to whisper during the Sunday service. A stern look from Mom always resolved the issue of who was sitting too close to the other. Although Dad did not attend services with us, he always provided each of us with a dime for the collection.

Then there was Reverend Huff and Anna May, his wife, who came to Rehoboth Church, and we all fell in love with them and their leadership of the youth. As kids of the youth group, we were many times asked back to the parsonage for popcorn and/or barbeque sandwiches. These were the most caring minister and wife I have ever known. We were at the church every Sunday evening and Wednesday Night for services. We were all so blessed by this young minister and his wife, who taught the youth how to read music and sing in a choir on Sunday mornings. When the family grew to welcome this baby boy named Timmy, the youth group became experts babysitters for him. Our hearts were broken when the Huff's were reassigned to another church, but we all knew we had been a part of something sent from heaven and far bigger than ourselves. We will be eternally grateful for the impact they had on our lives.

Just on the impulse of pretending to be sick and not able to attend church, Mother would only mention it to Dad, who made it very clear that if we couldn't go to church, we couldn't do anything else during the day, or he would kick our butts. (His vocabulary was a bit more explicit, but you get the picture!). In his own way, he did have the strong commitment to God that his children would be taught the Word, from little up, for which we are all grateful. But Mother was the rock of the family, always lending a hand to others and assisting the ill. Mother never turned a stranger away who came to our door. She offered food and water and gently reminded us that the stranger may just have been Jesus.

Often, we would have homeless men coming past our house after they had jumped off the train passing through Walnut Bottom. These were actual hobos and carried all their possessions in a little pouch on a stick over their shoulder. As kids, we were all scared to death of them, but Mom always offered them a seat on the porch, as well as water to drink, and usually a sandwich or leftover chicken and bread. What a saint she was and never had any fear for God was with her.

Mother had much to handle in getting us all up, dressed, and "clean" for church, but we were usually always there, singing in the choir and listening intently to the Gospel being taught by our devoted minister. I tried to choose the nicest flowery-print feed bag dress I had. Grandma Morrison kept and washed the feed bags, which carried the animal feed, and made them into dresses for me and my cousins. They were a bit stiff, but they were new and magnificent to me.

Louie was not always a happy camper about getting ready for church and would always be the last one into the car to head off to the services. You know, every hair had to be in place. He always got there in time and had so many friends he became everyone's buddy.

However devious Lou was, he was a skilled fisherman and hunter. His passion for trapping wild animals led him to design new ways to trap, and the money from fur trading helped him get his bike running. Once, however, he caught a skunk, and the odor was so atrocious Mother had to wash everything in tomato juice. What an uproar in the house and the neighborhood that created! It was one time when our mother was near her wit's end. After some weeks, however, it became a very funny story for Lou to tell his friends and cousins, Bob and Leon, in Camp Hill. At the ripe age of nine or ten, Lou decided to go to the creek and try his feet out with ice skates as the creek had frozen over due to the cold winter nights. Suddenly, the ice cracked, and Lou went into the freezing water. He slowly walked back to the house and stood outside, hoping his clothes would dry…ha ha…and by the time he decided he had had enough cold, he went into the house, where Mother found him standing by the door, clothes frozen tight to his body. Mother lovingly scolded Lou, then provided dry clothes and warm love to his shivering body. Within the week, Lou became very ill with a cold, and Dr. Allwein was called to the house. Pneumonia had set in, and Louie was very ill. Dr. Allwein always came to our house to treat our illnesses, can you imagine?

Boots and I shared a great passion for sending off to Hollywood to ask for autographed pictures of movie stars.

We scrapbooked everyone, and we both looked through the books starry-eyed at the beauty and magnificence of people and their lives that seemed to be light-years away from our little town. Their clothes and shoes were to die for, and Clark Gable was breathtaking in his black suit. Frank Sinatra was the most handsome man I had ever seen, and his voice was as smooth as velvet when we listened to him on the radio. Boots loved Frankie Lane and turned up the volume on the radio when he came on, then she would sing along. I would meticulously paste each photo into the scrapbook and dream...

Lou and Duane, as well as Lonnie, saved cereal box tops and sent off for Superman rings, baseball caps, and patches to sew on their shirts, stating they were members of the Royal Mounted Police Club and many others, all of which would be valued items if found today. This kept us busy, and we watched for the mail every day, hoping to get a letter or a small package. Times were simpler then. There were no toys, just a ball and stick used as a bat, a pair of roller skates, a ring, or a play watch out of the Cracker Jack box. We also had ice skates and would skate on the frozen creek during the winter. Sledding on the Bear's hill, behind our farm, was a very cold, windy, and errant event when the sled became uncontrollable. If we came sledding down the Bear's hill too fast and into the creek, or over it if the water had frozen, there were tricks to stopping in time. Sometimes, the older folks would build a bonfire in the evening along the side of the hill to warm our hands and feet. So magnificent, when we would huddle by the warm fire to thaw our frozen fingers and toes from the merciless winter wind and cold frost of the day.

The Bear family lived on a large farm behind our house and across the creek. They were very hard-working people, and their two girls, Betty and Doris, could pitch bales of hay as good as, or better than, any man around. They grabbed the bale of hay on the ground and pitched it to the top of the wagon to be taken to the barn for storage. One evening close to Christmas, Doris and Betty hitched their horses to the big polished wooden sleigh, adorned in red ribbons, and came to pick us up for an evening ride in the snow. It was the most magnificent thing I had ever done. We were wrapped in blankets, and the horses trotted around the fields in splendor. We laughed and shivered but were refreshed and exhilarated at such a fabulous, personal, unselfish Christmas gift, one I will never forget.

It is unimaginable to look back and realize that, as energetic and full of life as we all were, there was never a broken bone. Neither was there a TV set in the house since it had just been invented in the '50s. Therefore, Mother would sit us around the kitchen table and play games, such as bingo or checkers, with us until we started to argue. Mother never allowed playing cards, except for old maid, since she believed cards were of Satan and caused people to gamble and lose their way.

There was always a night or two a week when we would gather around the radio and listen to the clip-clop clip of the horses' hooves and the "Hi-Yo, Silver" of the Lone Ranger, who lead us to envision a notoriously endless rescue of a stagecoach from dangerous bandits wielding pistols and shooting wildly, trying to capture or rob the coach riders. As shots were fired, we all held our breath, grimacing in the hope that the Lone Ranger was safe. The Lone Ranger always came away from the fast-paced racing horses and stagecoach, gently holding a lovely damsel in distress, who was dressed in the finest lace and wide-brimmed hat. Every detail was explained by the animated voices on the radio.

Another night was spent making fudge or puffed rice balls and popping corn on the coal/wood stove until a heated discussion would erupt between one or two of us, stating that another one was eating all the fudge or popcorn. Oh, the lovely aroma of chocolate fudge cooking gently on the stove and popping corn that drifted throughout the house, reminding us that a very special treat was about to be partaken in when it was cool enough to eat. We sat munching popcorn or cereal, waiting to hear Mother's graphic stories of her own childhood memories of her family.

Mom would switch the conversation to her precious grandparents, whom she loved dearly, and who were now deceased. Her grandfather, Rev. Edward Perry, was a circuit minister, which meant that he traveled from church to church, preaching the Gospel. Mother related a story once in which her grandpa had preached prophecy that night at the church, and many had accepted the Lord, a most magnificent sermon. While traveling home in their buggy, a great bolt of fire landed in front of the horse, causing the horse to bolt with great anxiety. The fire then vanished, and the horse settled down again. Grandpa acknowledged that it was a message from God that great things had been done in the Lord's name that night and the end days were approaching. They were not to be afraid. There was not a cloud in the sky to suggest a storm that night, so Grandma and Grandpa Perry traveled on home to Scotland without a second thought. Many lives were forever changed by Grandpa Perry's faith and Gospel teaching.

Our house soon became Grand Central Station, especially during the summer months. Duane had earned a new Schwinn Bike, and Lou decided to use any spare part to recycle an old bike he had collected from someplace. He worked diligently repairing the bike and patching the tires until it was ready to ride. Lou and Duane always had friends from Walnut Bottom come over and swim in the creek that ran through the field to the rear of our house. There was no concern that the neighbor cows were in the stream not far away or that the water snakes swam near us. Lou tried to catch the snakes to bring to the house and frighten Mother to get a laugh or a shout out from everyone in the house. He was always the trickster and loved every minute. He kept the family laughing and sometimes crying in fright (like me).

It was hot, and all the kids came to swim in the pond of water that Lou and Lonnie had corralled by building a dam upstream, making it a swimming hole deep enough for swimming. Mosquito bites and poison ivy were the norm in our house. Measles struck one very hot and humid summer. We had to stay in a dark room to protect our eyes, and since there was no air conditioning, the windows were open in the event a breeze would pass through the room. The heat only made the measles multiply. The annoying itch was unbearable and eased only by a cornstarch dusting on our skin.

While I suffered from measles, Grandma Stum held her annual picnic in the meadow of the farm, which was adorned with grapevines and honeysuckle bushes, lending a magnificent aroma to the family gathering. Unfortunately, I was stuck in the darkened bedroom and could only watch the festivities through the window. How I longed for some of my mother's potato salad and Grandma's German slaw and rhubarb sauce; I could almost smell the fried chicken. Several large table cloths were spread out on the lush clover grass, and the food was placed in the middle. Family members came from everywhere to enjoy this festive time of year. We sat on the lovely soft meadow grass and enjoyed each other's food and conversation. We all enjoyed Grandma Stum's sisters: Sarah, Viola, Lorenna, Anna, Rosetta, Mary

Eva (Maime), and, of course, her brothers, Chester and William.

Grandma's lovely name was Ella Lenora. Beautiful names for such beautiful sisters, with warm and loving personalities to match. Prim and proper, as they were, with their aprons removed and dust caps of ruffles shielding their faces from the sun. Plain, long dresses, starched and ironed meticulously for an occasion like this one, white stockings, and white tie shoes were polished and neat. Laughter could be heard the whole way to my bedroom window, where I sobbed in disappointment. Uncle Chester was always being teased that he had grown out of his hair and was now bald; it never daunted the gentleman and his good-natured charm.

Our cousins would beg their parents to come and stay with us during the summer since there were so many kids around and always a "come what may" attitude with plenty to do in the country. Mom was so understanding and patient. Our house always had room for one more. Lou was always cooking up new tricks to play on the family and would walk into the freshly washed kitchen floor wearing his muddy boots, reeking of fish and stench from the creek after tending his traps along the creek. Needless to say, Boots did not appreciate these antics since she was the one designated to handle the house cleaning. She would then lock the door to keep the boys out, but anger would easily erupt and a windowpane was broken on occasion. When questioned about the incident, of course, it was always the other person's fault, so Dad would complain and put in the new pane with a stern warning that it better not happen again.

Lonnie spent a lot of time helping our grandparents on their farm since they were now aging and could not always respond to the issues that would arise. Grandpa always called him "Shadow," and Lonnie trailed along after Grandpa's every step, even imitating Grandpa's walk. He was just like a tiny shadow to our grandfather, who loved the company and teaching Lonnie how to milk a cow and farm. Lonnie became an astute follower of Grandpa's rules and mentoring.

Time passed, and Boots graduated from Shippensburg High School, a beautiful young woman, ready to begin her training in Carlisle Hospital to be a nurse. She worked very hard to learn the languages, especially Latin, and the medical terms and formulas for medicines, as well as worked part-time at the telephone company to pay for some of her expenses. Boots graduated from nursing school, and Mom and Dad could not have been more proud. Boots diligently washed and starched, then carefully ironed her crisp white uniforms and caps for her next week of duties at the hospital. They were so brilliantly white, clean, and fresh and were awaiting their turn to be worn and respected the next morning at the Carlisle Hospital. White shoes were polished every day and set to dry for the next day's nursing chores. We all knew who the nurses were and their rank at the hospital by the uniform they wore so proudly and respectfully. Times have sure changed.

Suddenly, one cold wintry night, a fire began to rage in the chimney that carried the smoke from the oil-burning heater in the living room. This and the coal stove used for cooking in the kitchen were our only sources of heat throughout the large house. Unfortunately, we were all asleep when Mother awoke to the roaring sound in the chimney. We all scurried to get outside, but Mother remembered Boots' freshly ironed nurse uniforms were hanging beside the fireplace to finish drying. The uniforms were salvaged after Mother's emotional outcry to the firemen, which resulted in no damage done, except to the fireplace and living room. We went to school smelling of smoke for a few days, but we were all safe, and Boots had a fresh uniform to wear to work.

Duane then graduated from Shippensburg High School and was a proud member of the High School Marching Band, in which he played saxophone. Duane even went to Penn State for a Band competition and always had a fondness in his heart for Penn State. A short story about Duane: he was in about fifth grade when the class was studying insects. Duane had a story to tell, so Mrs. Crider waited patiently for shy and quiet Duane to relay to the class that we had a lot of "piss-ants" outside, around the flower beds. Suddenly, Mrs. Crider quieted the class and reminded Duane that we don't use the term "piss-ants," that they are simply ants. Why should he not use the slang when that was all our dad and mom had ever called the pesky critters? It is fun to remember now, but I'm sure Duane was devastated since he was the "A" student and one of the favored ones in Mrs. Crider's class. Oh well, he never said it again.

Duane worked with our dad for a short time painting, then enlisted in the Navy along with our cousin Bob Jones. A very sad time for all of us, particularly Mother. She had depended on Duane for stability and always received a loving helping hand, no matter what the situation may have been. Duane was always there for her, quiet and intelligent, with a German knack for discipline, which we all grew to respect. He was a brilliant Navy electronics specialist, which led him to a degree from Villanova and a career with the Federal Government. Duane was discharged after four years of service and made it home in time for my high school graduation. What an exciting time for Mom and Dad, and a fantastic graduation surprise for me, that he was home and safe once again.

Louie started high school in Shippensburg, but then, due to redistribution calculations of the school board, he was required to transfer to the new Big Spring High School in his junior year. This move was not a pleasant experience for Lou since all his friends were in Shippensburg. Lou wanted to buy a car, so he secured a job at the bowling alley in Shippensburg, setting up pins until late at night. This caused him distress in getting up and on the school bus by 7:20 a.m. each morning. Lou has always been well-liked and very personable. He was a fantastic dancer at the Canteen, where we all went dancing on Saturday night in Shippensburg. Lou and I danced together a lot at the Canteen since he was comfortable with his friends there, and I didn't know anyone (I guess he felt sorry for me). We also went to the dance club in Newville occasionally and danced together—just because we could—until one evening, someone asked me if we were going together...I said, "Yikes, he's my brother." What a hoot! Don't get me wrong, I loved my brothers, but that was an awakening...

I finally graduated from Big Spring High School and used art as my choice of ambitions. Not a good move back in the day, but I also took typing and business classes. I was a four-year cheerleader and enjoyed dreaming of being a design artist or designer for all those Sears catalog displays! So much for that dream... Thanks, Tracy, Wendy, and Tanya, for completing this for me.

Lonnie also graduated from Big Spring and soon enlisted in the Air Force.

When Lonnie was eight years old, a huge surprise came to our home in the form of a new baby girl named Rebecca Susan. A year later, another wonderful surprise named Victoria Ann Louise arrived. They were the two most beautiful babies I had ever seen, pink and soft, and at the ages of ten and eleven, I was a little overwhelmed to have not one but two baby sisters. I was sure that was the end of babies in our family, but, sure enough, three years later, a darling little baby boy was born, and Mom named him Harlan Gregory. A second wonderful family had arrived, and we were now a family of eight children and two parents. We all loved having these new beautiful babies around to play with and try to keep them from growing up too fast. Of course, we must also remember our firstborn brother named Gerald, who only lived three days and died of pneumonia.

Mom went to work in the apple canning factory to add to our meager income, mostly working night shifts so she could be home with the little ones during the day. We all had chores to do when we were still living at home, so we did what we were required to do; sometimes it took some prodding from Mom or Dad, but we learned how to cook, clean, babysit, mow the lawn with a hand push mower (no motor involved); wash the clothes, and iron; plant and nurture the garden, and paint the sheds. When Dad would arrive home after a long day in the heat or cold, I was required to have dinner prepared for the siblings, and of course, for Dad. One night after I put Dad's dinner in front of him, he said, "Don't you know how to make anything other than fried potatoes?" I was embarrassed but soon learned how to make other dishes of his choice, like tomato gravy and cheese and pepper spread, along with ham and potatoes. But then, I was also trying to get Becky, Vicki, and Harlan ready for bed, homework done, and clothes pressed for school the next day, so I guess I wasn't too concerned about what to cook sometimes. Of course, I also had to excel in class and sing in the choir, as well as try out for the school play, just to prove I could…

When Duane was a young teen, he had persuaded Mother to get some chickens to raise. It seems he wanted Bantam chickens, which are smaller than regular chickens and many times stubborn and unruly. The rooster was beautiful, with feathers of many colors and a tall, colorfully feathered tail, which he strutted proudly with an attitude. However, he was always jumping at us when we were outside or when Duane tried to feed the chickens in the evening. One evening, the rooster flew up at Duane and "spurred" him sharply. In a second, Duane's normally slow to anger temper was provoked, and he struck the rooster with a board, which did the rooster in. So, we had the rooster for dinner. It was all over in a heartbeat, but we were now safe from the rooster. Duane never looked back and resolved the anger for the rooster in his own way, silently and methodically, going about his chores as usual.

Dad always raised pigs and beef for butchering in the winter, which fed our family for the coming year. Of course, Becky and Vicki were always with Dad when he went to feed the pigs in the evening, and it wasn't long until Vicki had named several of the pigs, with one, in particular, being named Pig Newton. Dad truly enjoyed the little girls and their banter about farming. Vicki was always willing to do what Dad required in feeding the pigs and making each little pig feel special. She was Dad's helper, and together they formed a bond that many of us envied, but that is just Vicki's caring and unselfish style.

Butcher Day came in November, usually over the Thanksgiving weekend, and the girls were in the kitchen preparing food for all the relatives who came to help with the butchering process. Cakes were baked in chocolate and yellow and carefully bathed in a sweet, sugary frosting for good measure. The aroma of freshly baking bread and sweet rolls encircled the farm like a lovely warm blanket. I hoped there would be leftover rolls for morning breakfast, which were left on the warming tray of the coal stove to mellow into the earthy goodness of yeast fermenting during the night. My goodness, they were so good, covered in Grandma's butter and Mom's scrumptious raspberry jelly made the previous summer.

Early in the morning, the pigs were singled out and slaughtered, one by one. Unfortunately, Pig Newton was on the list for slaughter. After the shots were heard, the house was filled with sobbing and sniffling at the loss of Pig Newton. Even our mother found tears running down her cheeks, but she warned Becky, Vicky, and Harlan not to feel sorry for the pigs, or they may not die quickly! Well, she had to tell them something to ease their pain.

The rest of the butchering day was filled with excitement at chopping meat and cooking the puddin' and scrapple, stirring the heavy iron kettles filled with all kinds of spices and scraps of meat. The lovely smell of cooking pork and brown sugar was spectacular. The bits left in the pot, called cracklins, were eaten and savored by all. Hams, bacon, and shoulders were rubbed with a wonderful mixture of salt, pepper, brown sugar, and some other spices; then, they were hung to cure in the cold cellar. Anyone entering our house during the entire winter months could detect the sweet aroma of hams curing. A real country kitchen blossomed when the hams were sliced and cooked with potatoes and green beans, along with a slice of warm apple pie. Even the neighbors knew what we were having for dinner when the sweet smell of fried ham drifted across the street. Oh yes, don't forget that when we baked a cake, we had to lay the eggshells on top of the stove or refrigerator so the cake would rise... Oh, the memories...

Rebecca (Becky) became the little mother to Vicki and Harlan, and Mother treated Becky and Vicki like twins since they were born twelve months apart. It was so cute to see them dressed alike and always together. When Vicki was bitten by a snake in the front yard, we all thought Becky was going to have a meltdown. She was so concerned for her baby sister. But it all turned out well. The two girls were trained to sing by a voice teacher Mother managed to hire. Their lovely voices were heard and appreciated many Sundays at Rehoboth and surrounding church services. Mom and Dad were very proud of the girls' accomplishments, and Mother supported them with love and prayers. Becky also became a cheerleader for Big Spring during her high school years. Vicki followed in Boots' footsteps and loved the nursing, caring field at Chambersburg Hospital. Vicki has always been the loving and caring safety net for all of us. Becky is a meticulous organizer and gets the job done when the family calls. She is always available to assist any of us if necessary and has become a wonderful mother and grandmother.

Becky and Vicki were devoted youth group leaders and church workers. Harlan was quiet and shy but always seemed to get into trouble when he was around his sisters. He was a fun and curious little boy, enjoying his neighborhood friends' visit to play. As a four-year-old, Harlan and Jessica, his niece (who was born a month apart), were always together outside, chasing the chickens or looking for bugs. One Easter, they were presented with baby chicks to care for and feed. During the act of loving the chicks so much, one of them was squeezed to death and had to be buried. A sad day for Harlan and Jessica, but no more baby chicks came to the house after that incident. A difficult lesson to learn.

Since Becky, Vicki, and Harlan were what we referred to as "the second family," they were treated to many amenities "the first family" never experienced, but the older family members certainly enjoyed having smaller siblings. As Becky and Vicki sat most of Christmas Eve on the living room steps watching for Santa, Mother was finally able to enjoy these little ones and share their excitement for the holiday season.

Yes, we were a poor family by financial standards, but we never accepted charity since our mother always provided, and the Lord richly blessed us. We never considered ourselves to be poor since other families were much worse off financially, and we were given ethics and morals as well as a wonderful Christian background by a loving, caring, unselfish Mother. She was so proud of each child and what they had accomplished in their lives that everyone who visited her in the Shippensburg Healthcare Center during her last years heard compelling stories about each of us. Oh, how she loved her family and could not wait to see each of us visit. Mother read her Bible every day as long as her eyesight permitted and prayed for each and every family member daily. Without her strong commitment to her faith, I know our family would not have grown to be this wonderful, caring band of brothers and sisters, aunts, uncles, cousins, grandchildren, great-grandchildren, and great-great-grandchildren.

Mother is now absent from the body and present with the Lord, but she has left us with a forever legacy to love the Lord with all our mind, body, and spirit, so we can all rejoice together someday in glory.

Oh God, how great Thou art. Thank You, Tanya.

Conclusion

Sharing these fabulously blessed family anecdotes has been a joy. There are so many other stories to add, and we need to do a book about the grandchildren of our beloved mother sometime. The family is a blessing from our Heavenly Father due to the prayers and sacrifices of our mother for so many years. It is my prayer that we will all stay in touch and, perhaps, be able to leave such a legacy to our own families.

I was handed a note from Terry as I pondered this writing with "Lessons we should learn from the 3 Nevers of Hulda":

"I knew Hulda for fifty years, and shortly after meeting her, I knew she was a caring Christian woman. Later in my years, there were '3 Nevers' in Hulda's life that I thought we could all learn and live by:

1st Never—During the fifty years I knew Hulda, I never heard her say a bad word about anyone, *never* (lesson for all).

2nd Never—I never saw Hulda angry. I'm sure raising eight very active children caused her many moments, but I *never* saw anger. Her gentle, caring, and Christian beliefs never allowed her to show anger (lesson for all).

3rd Never—I *never* saw Hulda have any hobbies. Then, I started to think, for a lack of a better word, Hulda's hobbies were her *family* and her church. Hulda *never* seemed to get caught up in worldly things. Her world was *her family* and *her church* (lesson for all).

As years passed, I grew to love and respect this tiny, gentle, caring Christian lady, and if we all try to learn her '3 Nevers,' the world will be a better place, and we will all surrender to the peace and tranquility Hulda shared with all who knew her."

Appendix

Family Members

Beulah (Boots) Lenora Baum married John Baum

Garnet Duane Stum married Judy Mohn (divorced) and
Doris Marks

Dorras Louis Stum married Lily Rife

Patricia Kay Stum married Terry Arbegast

Lonnie Stum married Martha Nelson

Rebecca Susan Stum married Chris Etter (divorced)

Victoria Ann Louise Stum married Larry Mathna

Harlan Gregory Stum married Penny Helman

Grandparents: Johnson

John Albert Johnson

Beulah Blanche Perry-Johnson

Great Grandparents:

    Flickinger Johnson and Rebecca Rowles Johnson

    Edward Perry and Anna Coy Perry

Grandparents: Stum

    James Elmer Stum

    Ella Lenora Gussman-Stum (Children listed below)

Great Grandparents:

    Edgar Henry Stum and Lucy Amelia Throne Stum
    (Children listed below)

Great-Great Grandparents:

    Samuel Throne and Elizabeth Tritt

George Louis Gussman and Martha Elizabeth Pisle Gussman

> George's Father: William Gussman, Elizabeth's Father: John Pisle. Mother: Sara (Snyder)

2nd wife: Alice

> Children: Charles Henry, Edna Viola Moffitt-Bowl, Anna Mabeth DeGroot, William LeRoy, Mary Eva Yoder, Lorenna May Goodhart, Ella Lenora Stum, Rosetta Julia Noggle, Sara Elizabeth Wolfe, Lewis Chester Pisle Gussman (Zora).

Children of James and Ella Stum (Our Grandparents):

> Louis Edgar Stum (Hulda Johnson), 9 children
> Miriam Blanche Stum-Jones, 4 children: Gladys, Albert Richard, Robert, Leon
> Fleta Alverta Stum-Morrison, 4 children: Mary, Robert, Richard, Linda
> James Kenneth (DorothySheaffer), 4 children: Kenneth, Barbara, Harry, Debbie

Children of Edgar Henry Stum & Lucy Throne (Trone) Stum: Dad's Grandparents

> Catheryn (Katie) (Amos Souder)
> James Elmer (Ella Lenora Gussman)
> Margaret Ellen (Phillip Thumma)
> Samuel (married to Native American)
> Mary

Henry Stum, Dad's Great Grandfather's Children

> Edgar Henry (Lucy Throne)
> John, Cyrus, Ann, Ell(en), Carry, James, Elizabeth.

Stum Foods and Things to Make You Laugh

Rock Candy on a String (wonderful hard clear candy pieces with a white string running through each piece).

Potato Candy—leftover mashed potatoes mixed with 10X sugar, rolled out and spread with peanut butter, rolled into a jelly roll, chilled, and sliced. Yummy…

Snow Ice Cream—Mom went upstairs, opened the window over the front porch, scraped some of the new snow away, then piled the underlayer of snow (which was clean!) into a large bowl, hurried downstairs, mixed in some sugar, and vanilla, and… Oh, what a treat for poor little kids.

Cracker Soup—Saltine crackers mushed by our fingers into a cereal bowl, then topped with warm milk and a bit of sugar.

Vanilla Milk—Into a large glass of milk, add a spoonful of sugar and a dash of vanilla. Stir a while, then enjoy.

Mush—Cornmeal cooked with water until thick. When cool, slice thin and fry in a bit of lard until crispy around the edges. Place on a plate and spread with butter and molasses.

Puddin'—All the leftover parts of the pig on the butchering day cooked together with pepper and salt. When cooked and formed in a loaf pan, remove and slice in a skillet to warm and fry a bit. Then, spoon over pancakes for breakfast.

Games

Button Button, who's got the button: One person stood up and turned their back on the rest of us who were seated at the table. We would pass a button from hand to hand under the table for a bit, then the person standing said, "Button, button, who has the button," and everyone would stop passing. The standing person would turn back to the ones seated and try to guess who had the button.

Marbles: The boys would form a small circle and have many small marbles scattered in a ring. Each boy had a "shooter," which was a larger marble, placed between the top of the thumb and the index finger. The shooter tried to hit as many small marbles in the ring as possible to keep or trade later.

Grandma Stum's Sally Lunn Pie

Line a pie pan with an unbaked crust and crimp the edges.

Place a cup of brown sugar over the inside bottom of the crust.

Pour about ¼ to ½ cup of milk or cream over the sugar and add about a tablespoon of butter that has been chopped into pieces. No need to mix, just bake at 350 degrees for about twenty-five minutes or until it looks done.

This was a favorite of all the Stum kids when Mom was baking pies. She would save the dough scraps and make a crust for this delicious pie... A very special treat.

Another Great Family Favorite Is Creamed Rice (A Dessert):

Cook one cup of rice according to package recommendations. Cool. Add ¼ cup of milk, ¼ cup of sugar, and one teaspoon of vanilla. Mix thoroughly. Cover and refrigerate overnight.

The next day, using one quart of heavy whipping cream, whip with an electric or handheld mixer slowly and add into the cream about ½ cup of confectioners' sugar. Whip until soft peaks form. Gently add the rice to the whipped cream mixture and chill.

These are just a couple of Mom's recipes, which we are handing down to the grandchildren, and items the sisters always make for family picnics and reunions.

P.K. Arbegast

Patricia K. Arbegast

Mother and Father of the Family

Louis Edgar Stum—Electrician's Mate—Third Class, U.S. Navy. DOB: 10/30/1910–DOD: 07/24/1972

Hulda Rebecca (Johnson) Stum. DOB: 12/01/1911–DOD: 05/19/2010)

This is our grandmother Stum. Ella Lenora (Gussman) Stum—DOB: 6/28/1889—DOD: 6/03/1960

CPSIA information can be obtained
at www.ICGtesting.com
Printed in the USA
LVHW050902140122
708387LV00014B/1148